A TREATISE ON HEAVENLY MINDEDNESS

MINDEDNESS

by Thomas Jollie

COPYRIGHT INFORMATION

A Treatise on Heavenly Mindedness by Thomas Jollie
Edited by C. Matthew McMahon and Therese B. McMahon

Published by Puritan Publications
A Ministry of A Puritan's Mind
3971 Browntown Road
Crossville, TN 38572
www.puritanshop.com
www.apuritansmind.com
www.puritanpublications.com

This Print Edition, 2015
Electronic Edition, 2015
Manufactured in the United States of America

ISBN: 978-1-62663-117-5
eISBN: 978-1-62663-116-8

TABLE OF CONTENTS

MEET THOMAS JOLLIE
Edited by C. Matthew McMahon, Ph.D., Th.D.

Thomas Jollie (1629-1703) is one of those puritans who is relatively little known, but ought to be better known. God's use of this man still reaches into the church today as we look to see the wisdom that he preached and penned from Christ's holy word for the good of the people of God.

Jollie was born of pious parents and was blessed with a religious education. His parents sent him to Trinity College, Cambridge, after he had religious convictions concerning salvation and Jesus Christ at a very young age. He was, "brought into a greater knowledge concerning things of the Spirit," during his learning there, and such convictions grew and abounded. He said, "Though my parents and education were pious, yet you little know what an abominable spirit did lurk and work in me under all. The Lord provided for my subsistence in Cambridge. He had been dealing with my conscience before, but there more fully. I had a zeal to the ordinances and for the cause of God; but much of it was common fire and not fire of the sanctuary. I had an inclination to the ministerial office, but there was too much precipitancy, in my coming from the academy and entering upon that work, being raw in years and rude in parts, and but poorly principled and furnished for such an employment. My own unfitness, and the greatness of the work were much hid from me." This occurred in conviction around 20 years old. After his conversion he was called to Althome where he ministered with his brothers for the good of the Gospel.

After this, he was unanimously invited by the people, to accept the pastoral office there. God was pleased to crown the labors of his servant here with his blessing, especially at the commencement. After a few years, he met with some degree of opposition, as most ministers do in some form or another, by attempting to establish a degree of discipline in the church.

The ardent spirit of Thomas Jollie could not be confined within the narrow limits of his particular charge at Althome. He also ministered in the surrounding counties and willingly cooperated, with his brethren in the ministry to promote the increase of spirituality among their respective charges in the adjacent counties. At their desire, he wrote a piece, entitled, "Evil tidings," concerning the Lord's withdrawing His presence, its causes, and such, and the substance of this he delivered in a discourse before the Savoy assembly in 1685. From that time on he because a public character in the churches employed in recommending ministers to destitute congregations, assisting at ordination, settling deputes, and striving to promote peace and union among those of different church order, but who agreed in the faith of the gospel.

Jollie suffered for Nonconformity. What he

endured for conscience sake, during twenty years, will appear from the following narrative, drawn up by himself.

"Through the good hand of God upon me, I was brought to Altham, in the hundred of Blackburn, in the county of Lancaster, with the unanimous consent of the people; and there blessed with good success in my ministry, for the conversion of many souls, until the year 1660; then the persecution against me began, merely upon the account of my nonconformity, before the last act of uniformity." "My first trouble was upon the 22nd of November 1660, by a warrant from three deputy-lieutenants, who brought me to Preston. There captain Nicholas Bannister of Altham brought me before the deputy- lieutenants, charging me with many things, mostly unjustly; and they put the path of Supremacy upon me, who was never suspected to be popishly affected. The design of the said captain Bannister, with other debauched young gentlemen of the country, failing in the aforesaid particular, upon the 15th of February following I was taken prisoner again by some of their soldiers, and detained for some time, to my great grievance and damage, in regard of the desolate condition and bitter lamentation to my people, the extremity of the weather, and the rude carriage of my guard. Being set at liberty, I was upon the 7th of March following, violently shut out of the public place by the said captain Bannister against whose illegal violence, when I sought relief from the Lord-lieutenants, I could get none." Such trials Jollie would endure time and time again for his preaching. Year after year he was accused and tried of being in some way illegal, then held against his will for a considerable time, then freed. He was over and over accused of false claims and the magistrates attempted to revoke his ordination, but at every turn the Lord was with him. When the five-mile-act was given he was forced to be removed from among his friends, where he became ill and had terrible pains and sufferings. He was even given a warrant to be banished from the three kingdoms. Reputable friends rescued him from this and sent him to another part of the country to reside in some form of peace. He was fined a number of times with monies beyond his means, and his goods were taken, where again, he would have to rally his people behind him in order to gain them back.

The remainder of his days appear to have been spent in peace. He lived to see the dawn and progress of religious freedom in this country; and in 1688, that ever memorable year, built a place of worship on part of his own estate at Wymond houses, near Clithero, where he continued to labor to his death. On the outside of the building is this inscription, "Luke 7:5, "For he loveth our nation and he hath built us a synagogue." Adjoining this place of worship is the house which Mr. Jollie built, and in which he lived and preached after his ejectment from Althome.

The character of Mr. Jollie was such as every Christian minister should strive to attain. He was very serious and exemplary, both in his private and public conduct, and was not ashamed of being called a *Puritan*. He was steadfast to his principles of faith and practiced. This sometimes exposed him for a season to the shiness of friends, and the determined opposition of enemies; but he would rather endure any outward troubles, than the inward distractions of an accusing conscience. His natural and acquired abilities were of no mean standard; they were diligently improved by application, and sanctified by the Spirit of God to the good of men's souls. Like many of the pious nonconformists he excelled in prayer, and was frequent in observing days of fasting and self-examination. His sermons were well studied, full of sound divinity and evangelical experience, and admirably adapted to promote real religion in the souls of his hearers. They were delivered with much energy and affection, were frequently watered with many tears, and were made exceedingly useful to arouse the careless sinner and comfort the distressed believer. His sentiments of church government were Congregational or Independent; but he was no bigot, he loved all those, "that love our Lord Jesus Christ in sincerity." His superior abilities, active spirit, and humble deportment, raised him to a high degree of esteem and influence in the churches of Christ, which he directed to the general good and the glory of God. The veneration in which he was held by those who knew his worth increased with his age, and his death was deplored as a great loss. His friends had this consolation, that he left behind him a son who possessed much of his father's spirit. This was Mr. Timothy Jollie, who acknowledged Mr. Oliver Heywood as his spiritual father, was ordained at Sheffield April 25tb, 1681, in very threatening times, and was very successful in training up young men to the work of the ministry in the academy at Attercliff.

CHAPTER 1:
The Doctrine of Being Heavenly Minded

Heb. 11:16, "But now they desire a better country, that is an heavenly; wherefore God is not ashamed to be called their God: for he hath prepared for them a city."

The apostle is here showing the blessed use the holy patriarchs made of their call out of their own country, and their wandering condition: *viz* the minding of heaven and making them heavenly. They were partly drawn, and partly driven to it. The issue of God's dispensation towards them was that they actually performed what they openly profess. Therefore we shall observe, the following doctrine.

The DOCTRINE: The blessed end, or event, of the saints' holy calling out of the world, and their afflicted condition in it is,—that they are heavenly both in profession and practice.

I. We shall explain the expressions in our text.
    1. God calls his people out of this world into another by his grace, and constrains them too. He did

this to Abraham and the rest of the, patriarchs. He called them from their idolatrous, profane kindred, out of their native countries. HE called them out of their former condition but especially out of that course of life they lived in, to another and better country, condition, and course. "Look unto Abraham your father, and unto Sarah that bare you: for I called him alone, and blessed him, and increased him," (Isa. 51:2). "Wherefore, holy brethren, partakers of the heavenly calling, consider the Apostle and High Priest of our profession, Christ Jesus," (Heb. 3:1).

This calling is by the grace of God. As he graciously appeared to the patriarchs, offered better things to them, and moved upon them by His Spirit; so he allures them that they can say, "Immediately I conferred not with flesh and blood." It is grace that draws you to him, and draws you after him. He constrains his people by a holy, violence; being merciful to them he catches hold of them, as he did of lingering Lot. Such is our infirmity, and such a hold the world has of us, that, "the lord said unto the servant, Go out into the highways and hedges, and compel them to come in, that my house may be filled," (Luke 14:23). As one observes, "To deal with some men, one had need bring a divine, a lawyer, and a soldier also." This is done generally by affliction, inward or outward. Usually this is the way of God both by his word and providence, "Therefore, behold, I will hedge up thy way with thorns, and make a wall, that she shall not find her paths. And she shall follow after her lovers, but she shall not overtake them; and she shall seek them, but shall not find them: then shall she say, I will go and return to my first husband; for then was it better with me than now," (Hos. 2:6-7). All this is to work out the horrid guilt of sin, and the hard servitude under it. Sad losses and crosses in the world ever drive us to God at first, and after him all along.

In coming out of this world and pursuing another, the people are partly free and partly forced. They are willing, as these patriarchs, who, "if they had been mindful of that country from where they came out, they might have had opportunity to have returned." The first saving work is to make us "willing in the day of his power," so all along, "if there be first a willing mind, it is accepted according to that a man hath, and not according to that he hath not," 2 Cor. 8:12. The nature of the soul is changed, and the nature of the state they are called into requires it. They are partly forced also. There is a necessity on them as well as a liberty in them. At first they are urged out of themselves unto Christ, and out of the world unto heaven. So it was with the prodigal, his own poor perishing condition worked on him as well as his father's fullness. Such is the nature of some that they need much more dealings like this from first to last.

2. The saints must be heavenly both in profession and practice, according to the state to which they are called. They are called from this earth and so from bring earthly they are called to heaven and so they must be heavenly, "As he which hath called you is holy, so be ye holy in all manner of conversation; because it is written, be ye holy; for. I am holy," 1 Peter 1:15-16. Saints should be heavenly as the state to which they are called, "As is the heavenly, such are they also that are heavenly. And as we have borne the image of the earthy, we shall also bear the image of the heavenly," 1 Cor. 15:48-49. They must be actually minding and pursuing heaven, not merely talking or pretending, but their word and way must declare they are for heaven. "If ye then be risen with Christ, seek, those things which are above, where Christ sitteth on the right hand of God,"

Col. 3:1. A heavenly frame and conversation are indispensably necessary.

3. This is the end designed by God. As it is the end of God in our calling; so it should be ours also: the end is most profitable, and the means is most proper. This is typified in the Lord's bringing his people through the wilderness, that they might be molded for the promised land, "Who fed thee in the wilderness with manna, which thy fathers knew not, that be might humble thee, and that he might prove thee, to do thee good at thy latter end," (Deut. 8:16). God always has the end in his eye, making us prepared for heaven; and he knows what dispensation will work best to that end. We were of a worldly frame and conversation, but now we give, "thanks unto the Father, which hath made us meet to be partakers of the inheritance of the saints in light," (Col. 1:12). In this way he works us up for the heavenly state, as a potter prepares his vessels of honor, "That he might make known the riches of his glory on the vessels of mercy, which he had afore prepared unto glory," (Rom. 9:23). God attains the end he aims at.

II. We shall illustrate the doctrine by some instances.

1. Does God take us away from our earthly relations, or take them away from us, and do we inquire what this design does and do for us? It is to deaden us to worldly relations, and quicken us to heavenly. There must be a divorce from them, yes, a death to them, in a sort, and our hearts must be set upon better relations, "And he stretched forth his hand toward his disciples, and said, behold my mother and my brethren! For whosoever shall do the will of my Father which is in heaven, the same is my brother, and sister, and mother," (Mat. 12:49-50).

2. Does he take away any accommodation in this world, or its comfort? You are not to have the thing to enjoy, or its comfort of it, that you may have more of heavenly enjoyments, and the comforts of the Holy Spirit. How many have not the *comfort* of the things, though they have the things themselves? His design in this dispensation is that his people by faith may have "the evidence of things not seen," and, "the substance of things hoped for," to comfort them.

3. If he blasts a man in his particular calling, or in his particular occupations in this world, is it not to mind him of his general calling, and bless him with spiritual blessings? Those matters took him off better

things, or turned him out of his course; but now, with Paul, he runs with full speed, and reaches with all his might, after, "the mark of the prize of the high calling."

4. If the Lord afflicts you in the health of your body, or in the gifts of your mind, it is to prevent some worse evil, and that your soul may prosper in grace. The spirit is apt to take up with its inn in the body, if it is comfortable, until we are made to groan under some distemper; then we cry out for, "our house which is from heaven," and for our being, "with the Lord." Gifts of the mind, as the blossom, must die away that grace, as the fruit, may remain.

5. If you are turned out of your habitations or estates, it is that you may dwell in God and with him; that you may have a better substance, and it have you; that you quit these moving tabernacles for eternal mansions, and that the spoiling of your goods here, may make you take notice of a better treasure hereafter. If you are turned out of your native country and native liberties, what is it but that you may come to a better country, that your hearts be set upon heaven, and that you be free in the New Jerusalem? As it was to the patriarchs, so to us that mind this better country, this

heavenly Canaan, this, "Jerusalem which is above," and, "which is the mother of us all."

6. Does God beat your off of your outward business and pleasures; is it not that you may you're your conversation and commerce in heaven, and solace yourself with the pleasures at his right hand? So Paul as a prisoner could say, "Our conversation is in heaven: from whence also we look for the Saviour, the Lord Jesus Christ," (Phil. 3:20). God found him business in heaven, and he could sing in prison on account of this expected deliverance.

7. If God does not breathe on your endeavors to do good or prevent evil, it may be you may shortly escape the evil to come and enjoy thy reward. "Then I said, I have laboured in vain, I have spent my strength for nought, and in vain; yet surely my judgment is with the Lord, and my work with my God. And now, saith the Lord, that formed me from the womb to be his servant, to bring Jacob again to him, though Israel be not gathered, yet shall I be glorious in the eyes of the Lord, and my God shall be my strength," (Isa. 49:4-5). "Merciful men are taken away, none considering that the righteous is taken away from the evil to come. He shall enter into peace; they shall rest in their beds, each

one walking in his uprightness," (Isa. 57:1-2). We do not make an escape unless our Lord fetches us off; but if the work is at an end, the wages must not be needfully long.

8. If the Lord deprives us of his ordinances, or withholds his blessing, it may be to draw us up to the fountain that we may drink there. He knocks out the bottom of these cisterns because we are apt to stay too much at them. Though we often lack public ordinances, yet, we may by meditation, eat of the hidden manna within the veil.

9. Does the presence of the Lord depart, and does he take away his Holy Spirit? Is it not that we may follow him to his place, and be swallowed up in his Spirit? He retires to heaven that we may follow him there in our thoughts. Surely the Lord has very much left this world! O! that we may bear great voice from heaven saying unto us, "come up hither," (Rev. 11:12).

10. Are we depressed with grievous temptations from the world or Satan? It is to make us weary of this world and willing to be at rest: as Paul, who had, "a desire to depart and be with Christ; which is far better," (Phil. 1:23). We are loath to leave the world until we are well wearied of it. When we are beset with

devouring temptations, we seek out a way upward, and say, "Blessed are the dead which die in the Lord from henceforth: yes, saith the Spirit, that they may rest from, their labours," (Rev. 14:13). When storms rise then we cast anchor within the veil.

11. Does God disappoint and delay us, as to our seeing some good to the church here? It may be that we may have holy desires after its pure state here, and heavenly desires after its perfect state hereafter, "Ye are come unto mount Sion, and unto the city of the living God, the heavenly Jerusalem, and to an innumerable company of angels, to the general assembly and church of the first-born, which are written in heaven, and to God the judge of all, and to the spirits of just men made perfect, and to Jesus the mediator of the new covenant, and to the blood of sprinkling, that speaketh better things than that of Abel," (Heb. 12:22-24. This turns up all, and shews the blessed communion is begun here, and will be consummated in the other world. We would otherwise have heaven here, much mistaking both the thing and time. We would stay on this side Jordan, but God is better to us, having reserved some better thing for us, and resolved to prepare us for it. O that it may be said of us all, "But now they desire a

better country, that is a heavenly;" and are the servants of Jesus Christ, "in hope of eternal life, which God, that cannot lie, promised before the world began," (Titus 1:2).

The *Reason* to confirm this doctrine, why God takes such a course, and for such an end, are the following:

1. It is the good pleasure of God to appoint this course. "No man should be moved by these afflictions: for yourselves know that we are appointed thereunto," (1 Thes. 3:3). "We must through much tribulation enter into the kingdom of God," (Acts 14:22). That course the Lord takes with his people in general, yes, with every one in particular, is not only the result of his prescience and predetermination, but of his good will and great wisdom. Should he give an account of his matters? May he not do what he will with his own?

2. The promise of heaven appertains to us through such a condition. "If we suffer, we shall also reign with him. Blessed is the man that endureth temptation: for when he is tried, he shall receive the crown of life, which the Lord hath promised to them that love him. If so be that we suffer with him, that we may be also glorified together," (2 Tim. 2:12 and James

1:12 with Rom. 8:17). Eternal life and the heavenly kingdom are promised; but it is in such a way of duty, and this is full of difficulty. Abraham, "obtained the promise," but it was, "after he had patiently endured," (Heb. 6:15). In this way it is said of Christ, "Ought not Christ to have suffered these things, and to enter into his glory?" (Luke 24:26). Sure heaven is worth suffering such hardship, for the Lord means to try our esteem of it, by our suffering for it.

3. It is most proper to have a weary wilderness before a comfortable Canaan. Heaven is not only a reward for service, but a rest from suffering; we must first be troubled, then have rest. What a tossing these patriarchs were in, and their posterity also, until they came to the promised land. This was the fittest way to deal with the promised seed. With others the Lord dealt otherwise, so the seed of Ishmael and Esau came sooner and easier by their portions.

4. We are not prepared for our Canaan but by this condition. By war the soldier is fitted for peace; by a storm the traveler is fitted for home; by toil the laborer is fitted for his bed; yes, we are the better prepared by greater sufferings for a richer heaven, and it will be the sweeter to us when we arrive there, "For

our light affliction which is but for a moment, worketh for us a far more exceeding and eternal weight of glory," (2 Cor. 4:17).

5. In such a condition we have more experience of the world's *vanity*, and so it becomes more embittered to us. The Lord then speaks to us, as he did to the wise men who went in search of Christ, when "the star, which they saw in the east, went before them, till it came and stood over where the young child was. When they saw the star, they rejoiced with exceeding great joy, "(Matthew 2:9-10). After we have come through various conditions, seeing vanity, and feeling vexation in all, then we throw away all and run to him saying, "Verily every man at his best state is altogether vanity. Surely every man walketh in a vain shew: surely they are disquieted in vain: he heapeth up riches, and knoweth not who shall gather them. And now, Lord, what wait I for? my hope is in thee," (Psa. 39:5, 7). We must experience the world's vanity, or we shall not believe even the testimony of Solomon, yes, of, "a greater than Solomon."

6. With such a condition we have more experience of heaven's comforts, and so heaven is endeared to us, "For as the sufferings of Christ abound

in us, so our consolation aboundeth by Christ," (2 Cor. 1:5). In such a condition we are more capable of heavenly comforts, and by these we are allured to God. Though the sun goes down, and there is a smoking furnace; yes, a horror of darkness; yet, there is also a burning lamp. "In the world ye shall have tribulation: but be of good cheer: I have overcome the world," (John 16:33). At such seasons heaven comes down to us, to fetch us up there.

7. Such a condition is a great friend to our spirit, as it serves more to promote grace and duty. We need such spurs and rods, and God usually uses such means to this purpose. Was not David at the best when he was made to wander, and when he was reduced to such straits? Opposition raises noble spirits, "The kingdom of heaven suffereth violence, and the violent take it by force," (Matt. 11:12). This condition is the better friend to our better part; and would you not have it go well with you in your spiritual part?

8. It is a great foe to flesh, which must be subdued, and kept under. The flesh would keep our spirits and spiritual affections down, to our great loss, and so would give advantage to temptation, and much misery would ensue. As one observes, "Flesh is a party,

a suffering party, and so not fit to be a judge." It is at a mortal feud with the spirit, until it is mortified by the sufferings of Christ, as the great argument, and the Spirit of Christ, the great agent. Our sufferings also are of use; our heavenly Father knows we have as much need of, "manifold temptations," as of our "daily bread." "Affliction abaseth the world, abates the flesh, and abets the spirit," as one observes.

9. Such a condition is to make us more heavenly. It is apparent if it were otherwise, we should be much more tempted to take up our portion with the men of this world, who, "have their portion in this life." We do not have much of outward things, because they would make our salvation so much more difficult, "A rich man shall hardly enter into the kingdom of heaven;" and even as it is, "The righteous scarcely be saved." The warm sun sooner strips the traveler of his cloak than the rough storm.

10. If it were not for suffering, we should be apt to miss our way. In a suffering condition we take a direct way to heaven and God, and walk in those, "straight, paths for our feet." In a prosperous state we usually go much about, and there are many things to turn us out of the way. Affliction is like the shepherd's

dog, to bark at and bring us in. We should have our hearts well persuaded upon these considerations, because the way of providence is so dark at this day.

CHAPTER 2:
INSTRUCTION

Heb. 11:16, "But now they desire a'"better country, that is, an heavenly: wherefore God is not ashamed to be called their God; for he hath prepared for them a city.

USE: First, by way of Instruction. We should therefore learn this duty, that we freely subscribe and faithfully set in with God, whatever our condition may be, that we may the better take down this bitter cup, and take with this hard saying.

1. This is indeed to worship God, when other worship is but in show only. The word (*proskuneo*,) to worship, seems to be derived from (*pros*,) to, and (*kuneo*,) to adore; which is from (*kuon*,) a dog; and signifies to crouch as a dog at his master's feet. This we do in passive obedience, as well as in active. It is religion, indeed, when we are pleased with what God does, and only do what he pleases. In this way Abraham was brought to his foot.

2. This will tend to clear your spiritual condition, though your outward state is dark. As in a dark night a little light appears much; so in a condition

of distress, grace will appear *if there is any*. Perhaps, in a fit infirmity may the more appear, as in Job's case but yet his graces lifted up, their heads, and shined forth again in their orient colors.

3. This is the life of Christ. He had the same will and work with the Father, but it was in a suffering way: "For I came down from heaven, not to do mine own will, but the will of him that sent me," (John 6:38). "O! my Father, if it be possible, let this cup pass from me; nevertheless not as I will, but as thou wilt; He went away again the second time, and prayed, saying, O! my Father, if this cup may not pass from me except I drink it, thy will be done," (Matthew 26:39 and 42). This was the life of Jesus, and must be manifested in us. Some he calls to more, but all in their measure must follow him into the garden and to the cross; and more vital acts of this: life put forth themselves in such extremities.

4. It plucks out the very heart of trouble. The perverseness of our wills, and crossness of our sickness, it makes trouble to be trouble: therefore, self-denial is promised, in order to our right taking up of the cross and following Christ. This is the mystery of making our sufferings lose their sting: as there is a mystery of extracting the sweetness of all our comforts.

5. Then it is we have the blessing of the dispensation. When we are brought under subjection to God and fall in with him, then the dispensation is indeed sanctified, and we improve all to make us more holy and heavenly, "Submit yourselves therefore to God. Resist the devil, and he will flee from you. Draw nigh to God and he will draw nigh to you. Cleanse your hands ye sinners; and purify your hearts, ye double-minded," (James 4:7-8).

6. What can we get by standing out and struggling with God's dispensation, "Woe unto him that striveth with his Maker! Let the potsherd strive with the potsherds of the earth. Shall the clay say to him that fashion-eth it what makest thou? or thy work, he hath no hands?" (Isa. 45:5, 9). God will have the glory of his sovereignty, righteousness, and goodness too, when we have taken our course.

7. May not your condition be worse than it is? You have along with Job, received much good at God's hands, and not with Lazarus, received little evil. The course God takes with us has much of light and love in it, "Unto the upright there ariseth light in the darkness: he is gracious, and full of compassion, and righteous," (Psa. 112:4). The cloud has a bright side could we but

look on it. Remember, also, those who have carried themselves whose condition has been worse than yours. Many, who were much better than we have had a far worse condition; but how sweetly did they conduct themselves!

8. Consult your own experience, what good you have found in such to course. Zeno made the best voyage when he suffered shipwreck; so a believer does also: yet, in all his shipwrecks he does *not* make a, "shipwreck of faith and a good conscience."

9. All your comforts are but temporal, so are your crosses. They must make way for, and give place to, that which is eternal, "The end of all things is at hand," with us. We should therefore reckon on it every day. In this way Job acted in his suffering state especially, "All the days of my appointed time will I wait, till my change come," (Job 14:14).

The Second Use: *by way of Trial*, whether we can say it is so now, in any measure, that our hearts are set upon heaven, that we are sanctified as to our calling, and that our condition is blessed to us.

1. Is your life in heaven? If you are followers of those patriarchs, your root, from where you continually receive life, is there *viz.* Jesus Christ. Not only are you

born again from above, but you are a branch that *lives by union* to the root. It was too much for him to have his life bound up in his Benjamin.

2. Is your living there? "The way of life is above to the wise, that he may depart from hell beneath," (Prov. 15:24). It is the very element in which he lives, and when absent, he is like a fish out of water. While the heart is down in the earth, it is dead; "For to be carnally minded is death: but to be spiritually minded is life and peace," (Rom. 8:6).

3. Is your company in heaven? There is an innumerable company there, and going there. It was this that made Dr. Preston say, "I must change my place, but not my company." A man of higher birth and breeding may have occasion with his neighbors of ordinary condition and capacity; but he associates with persons in another town, who are more fit for conversing with him.

4. Is your commerce with heaven? The apostle Paul could say. "Our conversation (*or trade*), is in heaven." He was still sending and receiving according to the nature of that country. If a man goes to the exchange, it is not only for company, but upon business.

5. Is your treasure there? Is your bank removed there? Are you laying-out yourselves, and all you can do, so that you may receive it in another world, not expecting a recompense on earth? If your treasure is there, your hearts will be there also. Send your minds there, where they have their freedom, as the sparks fly upward. Nothing short of the heart set on heaven will clear the title to heaven. The mark of heaven, is to be made *heavenly*.

A Third Use, *to admonish us*. We who profess such a heavenly calling, and are put to it in such a condition, when we have our hearts no more in heaven, then our condition is so uncomfortable.

1. We are admonished of the actings of this sin. Let us see that we do not seek our heaven in unlawful comforts here. They do not pretend to this holy calling, who seek their heaven in the enjoyment of unwarrantable objects. "Stolen waters are sweet, and bread eaten in secret is pleasant. But he knoweth not that the dead are there; and that her guests are in the depths of hell," (Pro. 9:17-18). Professors art in most danger of missing it, in having their hearts taken up too much in lawful comforts. "Then I said, I shall die in my

nest, and I shall multiply my days as the-sand," (Job 29:18).

Beware of base compliances. They secretly can pretend to religion, who will swim with the stream, and comply with anything that they may get or save outward things. Of such the apostle complains, "As many as desire to make a fair shew in the flesh, they constrain you to be circumcised: only lest they should suffer persecution for the cross of Christ," (Gal. 6:12). "Many walk, of whom I have told you often, and now tell you even weeping, that they are the enemies of the cross of Christ, whose end is destruction, whose God is their belly, and whose glory is in their shame, who mind earthly things," (Phil 3:18-19). If you go down the stream with such, you are sure to be swallowed in the gulf with them. But professors are more in danger of resting in outward ordinances, which are only means, and imperfectly hold out heavenly things as we imperfectly receive them, "Not every one that saith unto me, Lord, Lord, shall enter into the kingdom of heaven; but he that doeth the will of my Father which is in heaven," (Matt. 7:21). Ordinances are to bring us to heaven, but are not to be our heaven.

Do not rest short of God. Most men take up short of him, in whom alone is the true rest, "They have gone from mountain to hill, they have forgotten their resting-place," (Jer. 50:6). Whatever is short of union with God, is falling short of his kingdom. Even God's own people are too apt to take up with little of him which is to be had here. "As for me; I will behold thy face in righteousness; I shall be satisfied when I awake, with thy likeness," (Isa. 17:15). The design of any taste we have that the Lord is gracious, or any enjoyment of the powers of the world to come, is not to be at snare to give us say *it is good being here*, but a cord, to draw us after the full enjoyment of God in heaven.

If you look for heaven we must also look to be heavenly. Many, like the foolish virgins, will be looking to *enter* into heaven, against whom the door will be shut. These that make heaven their end, yet do not mind the necessities for it, are not heaven-like as the gospel teaches, "For the grace of God that brings salvation hath appeared to all men, teaching us that, denying ungodliness and worldly lusts, we should live soberly, righteously, anti godly in this present world; looking for that blessed hope, and the glorious appearing of the great God and our Saviour Jesus

Christ," (Titus 2:11, 13). Our calling is heavenly, let us then see we are not earthly, but walking, "worthy of the vocation wherewith we are called."

2. We are admonished of the aggravation of the sin of not having our hearts more in heaven. Consider its infidelity. Alas! how little do we believe God's word concerning eternal, things, and what tends to it. As the things of God and heaven are believed, so we are affected. Has God said and done so much to persuade us to believe, and yet we act as if they were idle tales? Men will not believe what is said; as to this heavenly country, because they do not see it.

How indifferent do we sometimes appear towards God, notwithstanding we profess to desire the heavenly country. His expressions of love are very fervent, though ours are very cold, "Set me as a seal upon thine heart, as a seal upon thine arm: for love is strong as death – many waters cannot quench love, neither can the floods drown it; if a man would give all the substance of his house for love, it would utterly be contemned," (Song of Solomon 8:6-7). How can we say we love him, and yet long no more to be with him, and have our hearts no more in heaven? Such as we love; we would be ever with; if not in person, yet in thought and desire.

The sin is attended with much ingratitude. After all the, means to draw us, how much willingness do we show to be with him? "Do ye thus in this way requite the Lord, O! foolish people and unwise? Is not he thy Father that hath bought thee? hath he not made thee and established thee?" (Deut. 32:6). I think I hear the Lord complaining like this: *what could I have done more for you, and yet you have no better fruit for me?* Alas, what common frames wider peculiar mercies! How it grieves, when kindness is repaid, by unkindness?

The sin is also idolatrous. "Be astonished, O ye heavens, at this, and be horribly afraid, be ye very desolate, saith the LORD. For my people have committed two evils; they have forsaken me the fountain of living waters, and hewed them out cisterns, broken cisterns, that can hold no water," (Jer. 2:12-13). If we have any other heaven, we have another God before him; we change our glory, and a woeful change we make. God is jealous over his spouse, and heart-idols are observed by him and provoke to jealousy.

This sin is an evidence, of treachery. To act in this way while we profess such a calling is to violate our covenants with God. This is too much of Esau's temper, "Lest there be any fornicator, or profane person, as Esau, who for one morsel of meat sold his birthright. For ye know how that afterward, when he would have inherited the blessing, he was rejected: for he found no place of repentance, though he sought it carefully with tears," (Heb. 12:16-17). Can we be believers and not breathe after what we profess to believe? What, Christians, and not be crying out to be with Christ, but rather desiring to stay here! What, saints, and so little spirituality, and so ranch carnality!

It shews much self-security. God alarms us on every hand, but we put the day far in front of us. How does God make the calm sea and Jordan to fly before us, yet we sit still! How he gives us prospects and tastes of the good land, yet we despise and dally about it! "Yes, they despised the pleasant land, they believed not his word: but murmured in their tents, and hearkened not unto the voice of the Lord," (Psa. 106:24-25). Perhaps we were a little awakened under some common or peculiar calamity, but settled in our security presently after.

The Fourth Use, *to direct us into such a course and frame as are here described.*

1. See that God is our great end and way, and his Spirit our leader. Our language must be, "Thou shalt guide me with thy counsel, and afterward receive me to glory," (Psa. 72:24). God must be our all in all. He is the soul's resting place. To enjoy and honor God, is the last and everlasting end we have to propound to ourselves. This is heaven, when it is in perfection. Jesus Christ is the way, both to remove all obstructions out of the way, and bring us again to God, "Christ also hath once suffered for sins, the just for the unjust, that he might bring us to God," (1 Pet. 3:18). As the end of our desires must be right, "so also the ground of our hope." It is by the Spirit's direction that we must be brought to the heavenly country. The things of the other world are hid from us, but as the Spirit shows them, "God hath revealed them unto us by his Spirit," (1 Cor. 2:10). Indeed we cannot perceive them but by his Spirit, and when unknown they are often not desired.

2. We should see we are well grounded as to the certainty of eternal things. "He that believeth on the Son of God hath the witness in himself," as well as in the scriptures. We should prove we judge the excellency of these things, by not making light of them; but choosing the good part which shall not be taken

away. Let us see we are personally interested in these blessings, and be persuaded on good grounds. Interest endears anything to us; our home is homely to us, our country, though bare, is beloved by us: how much more such a kingdom, so gracious a mansion, and undefiled an inheritance?

3. We should observe our special hindrances, advantages, and arguments. "Let us lay aside every weight, and the sin which doth so easily beset us, and let us run with patience the race that is before us, looking unto Jesus the author and finisher of our faith," (Heb. 12:1-2). Some hindrances are more peculiar to some persons. What are the weights that hang on us, or the stumbling-blocks that lie in our way? As far as we can, let us shake off those, and get over these, "Go through, go through the gates; prepare ye the way of the people; cast up the: highway; gather out the stones; lift up a standard for the people," (Isa. 62:10).

10. All ordinances and means must be observed, and the various duties, both of our particular and general callings, must be attended to, as means of bringing us on our way to heaven, and becoming heavenly. The mark at which we are aiming must be always in our eye. A man will frame himself for his

work, especially considering he must be made satisfied before he can be made a partaker.

4. Let us not neglect any help we can receive, and ever be ready to catch the gales of God's Spirit. We may sometimes light our candle at the lamp of others, and we should never be above accepting help from even the meanest. All lawful endeavors must be used, and a man must chafe his own hands if he complains of cold: for we must not be too proud to make use of others, nor too slothful to bestir ourselves. The influences of the Holy Spirit must be peculiarly prized. How can we pass the seas without his gales? His blessed breathings must waft us into this better country, and by his hand we must be caught up into the third heaven. Pay attention to reading the word of God: for this will help the defects of memory. Meditate upon, these matters, not only occasionally, but frequently, and solemnly; this will make reading profitable; for while we muse our hearts will burn.

Discourse, if it is savory and serious, will help much, "Did not our heart burn within us, while he talked with us by the way, and while he opened to us the scriptures?" (Luke 24:32). We should discourse with God by prayer, with ourselves by soliloquies, and with one another by heavenly communion.

5. Improve opportunities, objects, and occurrences, to acquire heavenly-mindedness. What opportunities more seasonable than the Lord's Day? What objects more suitable than those before you in God's house? Here you have the very same objects, company, and employment as in heaven. Other objects may be improved, but these are your, harvest. What occurrences are more suitable than the disappointments we met with in this world, and the death of friends? Also improve those seasons when the Lord bows down his heavens, comes to us, and bestows the *influx* of his love.

The Fifth Use, for exhortation, to improve our heavenly calling and condition.

1. There is nothing else worthy your hearts. Be sure this world is not worthy of your hearts; for the heart of man is raised above the heart of other, creatures, and your, hearts are raised above other men's. You are born from above, and then you must live according to your birth. You are risen with Christ; then you must seek things above; things below are beneath you, but this object is most worthy, your noblest

powers. Here is employment for your most elevated affections. O raise up your, hearts, and praise God in the highest heavens, "Praise ye the Lord; praise God in his sanctuary: praise him in the firmament of his power," (Psa. 110:1).

2. It is a frame of mind worthy of a Christian, and is a witness to you. It is a frame becoming the gospel: it is your *excellency* to be heavenly: then your spirit and conversation are divine, and you draw towards the life of God. As the world is not worthy a place in such hearts; so the world is not worthy of them. God does not call to any privilege or performance, but he strengthens persons for the same. If you have such a frame of mind, it is a witness within you. A heavenly frame is a certain evidence, "Wherefore the rather, brethren, give diligence to make your calling and election sure; for if you do these things, ye shall never fall: for so an entrance shall be ministered unto you abundantly into the everlasting kingdom of our Lord and Savior Jesus Christ," (2 Pet. 1:10-11). This is the character of a Christian indeed, that he is a citizen of heaven.

3. If your hearts are raised in this way, it will be greatly for the cherishing of your graces, and comfort of

your lives. Every grace flourishes under the warm and watering influences of such a frame. Remember what Moses was, both as to his countenance and carriage, when he came down from the mount. It will also afford comfort to your lives. If God sets you at the upper end of the table, it will be of little comfort if he does not carve for you something of this better portion. Outward comforts are no comforts if they do not have a dash of this heavenly frame. If he puts you to it, as he usually does, how can you carry yourself comfortably through this weary world, were it not for some first fruits of the heavenly country? A heart raised into heaven, and ravished with its comforts, will abide much; the martyrs are witnesses to this. Such a frame is the life of our lives.

4. A heavenly frame will be a special preservative from temptation, and promoter of duty. Though the *tempter* is in high, places, you are upon the wing; of what matter then is the snare, you sit in heavenly places out of his gun-shot. When Paul came out of the third heaven, Satan set upon him; but, if you have "this helmet of the hope of salvation," you may lift up your head. It is also the never failing motive to duty. Philosophers talk of a perpetual motion, this is the

everlasting motive, and the Spirit is the everlasting mover. All temporal motives will fail us at one turn or another. You cannot carry on your Christian course without having, "respect to the recompense of the reward."

5. It will clear providences and content the soul. If we inquire why it is thus with the people of God here, we should remember there is something to follow; when we have looked awhile into eternity, the way of God's providence in this world is more explained: then, and not until then, we are content. A person in hope of a kingdom will be cheerful and content, though at present he may be hard put to it; so this is how David was in his weary condition, but, he must have a crown after all. In this way it was with the Apostle Paul, "We rejoice in hope of the glory of God. And not only so, but we glory in tribulations also," (Rom. 5:2-3).

6. The profit will redound to yourself. Heavenly-mindedness is a duty which brings much, of heaven down into the soul, and will have its reward hereafter. But the profit of this duty, is not confined to yourself, it will extend itself to others also. Like the sun you will shine in your orb, and shed light upon others.

7. Such a frame of mind, will, be a praise to your profession, and the promised land. O the power of that grace and glory, which makes you triumph over everything temporal! "Walk, worthy of God, who hath called you unto his kingdom and glory," (1 Thess. 2:12). To say, as David did in Psa. 56:4, is to bring glory to God, "In God will I praise his word, in God I have put my trust; I will not fear what flesh can do unto me."

The Sixth Use, for *consolation*. Comfort yourselves and one another with these words as persons usually do when far from home, and fare ill in a strange country.

1. Recollect there is a better country than, this, and yet many have not so good as this. The devils are in a woeful condition. There is no redemption for them: for as they had no tempter, they have no Savior. The damned in hell have no remedy now. O the misery of that country prepared for them! "Who among us shall dwell with the devouring fire? who among us shall dwell with everlasting burnings?" (Isa. 33:14). The condition of any living on earth is better than theirs: for the dispensation of the kingdom of heaven is not taken away from us *yet*. There is a better country for you than any gospel-land in this world, not confined to any

nation as the Jewish was, "We, according to his promise, look for new heavens and a new earth, wherein dwelleth righteousness," (2 Pet. 3:13). "As I lay sucking at my mother's breast, (Luther says,) I little knew how I should afterwards eat, drink, and live: even so do we as little understand what the life to come will be."

2. Consider the better country has the better part of you, and you have good ground to hope you have a part in the celestial Canaan. "Rejoice because your names are written in heaven," (Luke 10:20). That eternal life which is already begun in you, is an entrance upon the heavenly inheritance: you have reached the confines of that country.

3. Think of the cloud of witnesses passed before you, whom you are to follow in this world into another. Are you called out from your worldly relations to travel? So were they. Are you to go, "from one nation to another, from one kingdom to another people?" So were they. Are you oppressed under task-masters, and have you to wander through a weary wilderness? So were they. They are gone before you, not only through this "valley of Baca" to the mount Zion of a heavenly, conversation, but through the valley of the shadow of

death into this heavenly country. Are you better than they, or think you to do better than they? Then why do you think much of being called to walk in the same course, to that, "better country, that is, an heavenly."

CHAPTER 3:
THE FULLNESS OF REDEMPTION

Psalm 130:6, "With him is plenteous redemption."

The Psalmist being in depths of inward and outward trouble, raises up himself in faith and prayer, and waits in hope. He puts all the Israel of God upon the same course, and the arguments used are, that there is redemption enough for them all, and that there is a particular promise of redemption in the worst case, to wit, "from all iniquities."

THE DOCTRINE: As we have seen we are to be *heavenly-minded*, so we consider a high-minded biblical truth – that with the Lord is *plenteous redemption*. "We have redemption through his blood, the forgiveness of sins, according to the riches of his grace; wherein he hath abounded toward us in all wisdom and prudence," (Eph. 1:7-8). We shall inquire the following:

I. What this redemption supposes?

1. The great need, misery, and loss, which men in a natural state are under. If men are not in such a

case, then what need is there of such redemption? Is the Father prodigal and lavish of the blood of his beloved? Our happiness being lost, and we, laboring under vile bondage and dreadful condemnation, yes, *dead* in trespasses, need all help; and cannot savingly help ourselves in the least, yet cannot be quiet. This redemption shows us, that we need a thousand mercies, but cannot obtain the least deliverance or favor; that we are as captives sitting in ashes "in a dark prison house," or as, "prisoners in a pit, wherein is no water," and as "the prey of the terrible." O! the horror of such a condition!

2. It supposes that manifold dangers and necessities, temptations and tribulations, attend the people of God in this world. They have continual need of the redemption of the Lord; being plunged in depths, and their condition being poor, they are helpless from anything else but this redemption. Though so many deaths and destructions gape for them, yet are they as sheep led to the slaughter, that cannot rescue themselves; for their redemption is of the Lord, "Many are the afflictions of the righteous: but the Lord delivereth him out of them all?" (Psa. 34:19). We shall now discourse concerning God's redemptive hand.

II. Concerning the Redemption which is of the Lord. Here let us inquire the following:

1. What this redemption is from? It is a redemption from all evils, in God's time and way. Consider such high thoughts concerning this.

There is a redemption from a state of nature, from the curse, condemnation, yes, command of the law, in a legal sense, "Christ hath redeemed us from the curse of the law, being made a curse for us," (Gal. 3:13). "There is therefore now no condemnation to them which are in Christ Jesus who walk not after the flesh but after the Spirit," (Rom. 8:1). Jesus Christ came, "to redeem them that were under the law;" and henceforth they, "are not under the law but under grace," (Gal. 4:5, Rom. 6:14). Jesus Christ says to the adversary, "Deliver him from going down to the pit: I have found a ransom," (Job 33:24). Not only is there no law against them, but all law is for those for whom Jesus Christ has satisfied; so that he may say, do me justice for these souls, they must not be under a law-state or law-spirit. There is a redemption from the lordly and conjugal dominion of sin, though not yet from its being in us, "Thou shalt call his name Jesus; for he shall save his people from their sins," (Matt. 1:21). "Being made free from sin, and become servants to God, ye have your fruit unto holiness, and the end everlasting life," (Rom. 6:22). "Who gave himself for us that he might redeem us from all iniquity, and purify unto himself a peculiar people, zealous of good works," (Titus 2:14). In this work, there is not only redemption from that power sin has in us, by tyranny or love, but temptations are restrained and subdued by restraining and renewing grace. And what is not yet finished is reckoned as *done*; sin is dead and we are dead to it.

There is also a redemption from devils and men, so that we shall be servants of neither. Jesus Christ partook of our nature, "that through death he might destroy him that had the power of death, that is, the devil; and deliver them who through fear of death were all their life time subject to bondage," (Heb. 2:14-15). "Ye are bought with a price; be not ye servants of men," (1 Cor. 7:23). Saints are not left to the will of men or devils even in outward respects; and the scriptures seem to point at a binding of Satan and a deliverance from wicked men, before the end of all things is come. This may be such a deliverance as the church has not yet known.

There is a redemption from affliction and temptation, or from its evil, "He shall deliver thee in six troubles: yes, in seven there shall no evil touch thee," (Job 5:19). "I pray not," says Christ to the Father, "that thou shouldest take them out of the world, but that thou shouldest keep them from the evil," (John 17:15). Stay a little, and wonder at this redemption, should you never see any more than this. In such a thing we may be *more* heavenly minded.

But there is a second Redemption, a final Redemption. All evil shall then be perfectly and eternally done away, and a redemption from the grave, from condemnation in judgment, and from eternal wrath will be enjoyed. Many will be raised from the grave, who are not redeemed as the elect of God are; many will be raised with disadvantage, as to what they had: their worldly glory will not rise with them; and what will they endure for ever, when raised out of the grave and thrown into hell! But O! what redemption shall they say there is with the Lord, when the saints are raised to be with him! No remainders of sin and its fruits, nor of temptation shall appear; but the coasts will be forever clear. Let us rejoice before the Lord with our first-fruits, and when the day of redemption comes we shall have the joy of harvest.

2. In what does this redemption consist? It is a redemption of persons and things. Of persons. All in some sense partake of it except devils. Hell is stayed awhile, and the world enjoys many mercies, yes, has the means of more, and may be considered as bought for some servile use to the church. But we speak of them that are properly *the redeemed of the Lord* and for these, all positive good is purchased. The whole inheritance of privileges, the whole store and heap of blessings in the covenant, yes, all we have lost, all we can desire, want, or be capable of enjoying, are purchased for the saints.

It also includes a redemption, or purchase, of blessings or things. All the riches of grace are purchased by the Lord for his people. Who can number these riches of grace? Much rather, who can tell of their value but he that purchased them? What is union with such a head, or marriage to such a rich heir? There are the riches of justification and adoption, together with the blessings that follow. Such blessings are his Spirit dwelling in us; we dwelling in his house, and under his peculiar providence. A full inventory of the blessings of grace may be seen in, 1 Cor. 3:21-23, "All things are yours;

whether Paul, or Apollos, or Cephas, or the world, or life, or death, or things present, or things to come; all are yours; and ye are Christ's; and Christ is God's."

As to the riches of glory, only eternity can serve to tell over those vast sums, read over that inventory, survey that inheritance, or enjoy the perfection that attends that state, "When Christ, who is our life, shall appear, then shall ye also appear with. him in glory," (Col. 3:4). God will so deck his Son's bride, and make his glory arise upon her in the latter days, that it will be a heaven compared with her present condition; yet that state is only a preparation, or as the holy place, in respect of the holy of holies, "Eye hath not seen, nor ear heard, neither have entered into the heart of man, the things which God hath prepared for them that love him," (1 Cor. 2:9). The unborn child cannot apprehend what it afterwards knows, neither in its nonage perceive all the accomplishments, riches, and dignities of its adult estate. So in heaven, are things unutterable and unintelligible to us here; if it were not so, we might be tempted to break down the hedge, that we might enter that paradise.

3. The question is, *What this redemption is by*? It is by price. Price is related to redemption as sacrifice to

atonement, and penalty to satisfaction. *Price* is often called redemption. We were prisoners of justice, and the order of justice must be observed; all must come in a way of ransom, and purchase, through Christ, who, "hath loved us, and hath given himself for us an offering, and a sacrifice to God for a sweet-smelling savour;"—"that God might be just, and the justifier of him which believeth in Jesus." Many were redeemed before the price was laid down, but God took Christ's word, as if it had been already paid.

This redemption is obtained by power also. A work of mighty power is necessary for the obtaining, and maintaining of all our privileges; for the beginning and perfecting of the whole work: this is, "the exceeding greatness of his power to us-ward who believe," and we are, "kept by the power of God through faith unto salvation," (There is great need of kingly power; for sin, Satan, bad men, and the grave, will not easily let go: we must, therefore, be rescued by a strong hand, and be held by a strong hand, or they would fetch us back.

This redemption is obtained by the price and power which are in the Lord Jesus Christ. Our text says, "with him is plenteous redemption;" it is with the

Lord not with us. "Of him are ye in Christ Jesus, who of God is made unto us wisdom, and righteousness, and sanctification, and redemption," (1 Cor. 1:30). "We have redemption through his blood, even the forgiveness of sins," (Col. 1:14). As all the work is transacted by him, so all fullness is lodged in him; yes, he is our righteousness and strength.

4. What is this *plenty* of redemption which is with the Lord? The scriptures set it out by comparisons, as light in the sun, water in the ocean, or in a fountain: but, indeed, expressions and works of nature are too shallow, they cannot fully represent its plenty.

To add something to further the illustration of the plenteousness of this redemption, consider the fitness, fullness, and sufficiency of the Redeemer, both in his person and in all the parts of his work. He was "mighty to save" and was abundantly fit for it, "even to the uttermost." As God, he had the right of propriety over us, and power in himself; and as man, in such an office, he had the right of kindred and sufficiency, so that he could accomplish the office of a kinsman, "Their Redeemer is strong; the Lord of hosts is his name," (Jer. 50:34). "Thus saith the Lord, the King of Israel, and His

Redeemer the Lord of hosts; I am the first, and I am the last; and besides me there is no God," (Isa. 44:6). He is the *plenipotentiary*, has all power far the work, as to satisfaction held forth in his death, "The son of man came not to be ministered unto, but to minister, and to give his life a ransome for many," (Mat. 20:28). "The good shepherd giveth his life for the sheep. I have power to lay it down, and I have power to take it again," (John 10:11, 18). "The church of God, he hath purchased with his own blood," (Acts 20:28). "Christ loved the church, and gave himself for it," (Eph. 5:25). He is a suitable person for the place of Redeemer, if we consider his power to apply the benefits, of this redemption as held forth in his intercession: "Wherefore he is able also to save them, to the uttermost that come unto God by him; seeing he ever liveth to make intercession for them," (Heb. 7:25). Soul, do not be dismayed at what oppresses you, or faint at a sense of your need; for if you consider who your Redeemer is, and how he has gone through his work, you will conclude there is, "plenteous redemption with him."

What this plenteous redemption is may be further learned if we consider the redemption itself, but especially its gospel tidings. These will cause us to be more heavenly minded.

It is a redemption of more good than was lost, though not of all persons that were lost; this gift exceeds the offence. O rich redemption! that misses none for whom it was designed. Christ Jesus, "gave himself a ransom for all to be testified in due time," (1 Tim. 2:6). "The Lord redeemeth the soul of his servants: and none of them that trust in him shall be desolate," (Ps. 34:22). You may rest satisfied, Christ will see that none of his redeemed ones shall be lost. O rich redemption! that extends to, and comprehends *all* conditions, "The grace of our Lord is exceeding abundant, with faith and love which is in Christ Jesus," (1 Tim. 1:14).

This redemption not only works good to us out of our afflictions, but glory; yes, transcendent glory, "For our light affliction which is but for a moment, worketh for us a far more exceeding and eternal weight of glory," (It is a fountain for freeness, and a foundation for sureness; and as it is effectual, so it is eternal and cannot miscarry; it is from eternity with the Son, and to eternity with the saints), "For by one offering he hath perfected forever them that are sanctified," (Heb. 10:14).

Surely there is redemption with the Lord, redemption enough to redeem Israel from all his iniquities, and from all his troubles. This treasury is not like that of the Venetians, very large, but wastes by using; like that of the Spaniards, it has a root, a mine; yes, it passes them both; for the more it is used the more it increases.

The application of this redemption proves its plenteousness. The preparation and means are all provided in plenty, and are all ready, "And in this mountain shall the Lord of hosts make unto all people a feast of fat things, a feast of wines on the lees; of fat things full of marrow, of wines on the lees well refined," (Isa. 25:6). The servants of the Lord-are heard saying, "Come; for all things are now ready." Everything is now worked out, laid up, and ensured in Jesus Christ; he pours out his Spirit, endues and sends men, and gives them his message and blessing. Particular churches and their ordinances are full; the church is said to be, "his fullness," and all our springs are there, "They shall be abundantly satisfied with the fatness of thy house; and thou shalt make them drink of the river of thy pleasures," (Psa. 36:8). The objects and work prove there is plenteous redemption with the Lord. All persons in some sense partake of this redemption; for their temporal good is for the church's service, and for the honor and use of Jesus Christ our Lord. The sufficiency of this redemption is universal, and the tender of it is universal where it comes; but God's Israel according to election obtains it, "In the Lord shall the seed of Israel be ratified, and shall glory," (Isa. 45:25). Where this redemption is savingly applied, it works most free, it even works its own preparations; there is nothing in us to pre-dispose, but the whole is according to the good pleasure of his will, and by his almighty power.

III. We shall mention the reasons why this plenteous redemption is with the Lord.

1. The pleasure and design of God is that it should be so. "Even so, Father, for so it seemed good in thy sight: All things are delivered unto me of my Father," (Matt. 11:26-27). It is not only the pleasure of God it should be so, but it serves his design, which is the glory of his grace. To provide such plenty, and reserve it in the hand of Christ, shews abounding grace, yet in, "all wisdom and prudence," A little redemption-grace will not serve to show forth the divine glory, nor putting it into our hand, who are apt to embezzle and

pervert all: therefore he, "hath raised us up together, and made us sit together in heavenly places in Christ Jesus: that in the ages to come he might show the exceeding riches of his grace in his kindness toward us through Christ Jesus," (Eph. 2:6-7).

2. Our case requires, both in our natural and renewed state, that this plenteous redemption should be with the Lord. The soul and its salvation are so precious, that a little redemption, or much put into our hands will not be to any effect: for our sins are so many, justice is so infinite, our enemies are so great, and necessities so innumerable. Faith and hope cannot live on lower things, nor on little of better things, they must have *plenty*; and as our necessities require plenty here, so our capacities in heaven will *require* plenty. It must, therefore, be a great salvation, and, "plenteous redemption," with the Lord, for spirits made perfect.

The First Use. It shows where store and poverty are. The Spirit tells us the former is with Christ, and the latter is with us. All plenty of redemption is with the Lord Jesus Christ; we must look to him as stored with all fullness:, all power, infinitely beyond us, piled and built up forever, "For it pleased the Father that in him should all fullness dwell," (Col. 1:19). He is the great motive and mover both in heaven and in earth. I think all should lift up their heads in faith, and their fed in coining, at the first knel of this joyful sound.

All wretchedness and poverty are with us. We must see ourselves in this glass, and it is the most sure way of the most safe humbling. The doctrine points out the plenty of redemption which is in Christ, and by it shows what we are; as when the needle points to the north it also shows the south. The apprehension of our nothingness will send us to this fountain, and seeing we have no motive in us to move God, *except to wrath*; no power to move ourselves. We are drawn to hearken and come *to him* for this plenteous redemption.

The Second Use. It should teach us to examine what signs of interest we possess in this vast stock of redemption. Has the Lord let us see our need of redemption, and of its plenteousness? O what a sinful, damned, impotent, wretch am I! I have not the least mercy belonging to me, and yet a little will not suffice! "O wretched man that I am! who shall deliver me from the body of this death," (Rom. 7:24). If the Spirit is at work with us, he does not skip over his work; but first he convinces thoroughly of sin and misery in us, and then of all grace and righteousness in Christ. Again, is there a taking discovery of this plenteous redemption which is with the Lord? O what suitableness, fullness and glory in these things! What fast hold do they take of our hearts, and how do they take them off from other things! All other things are as nothing when compared with this redemption; yes, all power in us, with us, or against us is blasted, when a glimpse of this is let into the soul; and the mind will never be quiet until interest and communion be obtained, and an evidence of it enjoyed. Has your Redeemer looked in at the gate of your prison, awakened you, as when he smote Peter on the side, and having knocked off your bolts made you follow him? Examine further the following:

Whether or not your knowledge of this redemption makes you, "neither barren nor unfruitful?" Do you add to your faith, self-denial, love, and repentance, as Mary the weeper at Christ's feet? Does it wean you more and more from the world? Does it make you fruitful in the duties of all relations and conditions, as it did Paul? "God is able to make all grace abound toward you; that ye, always having all sufficiency in all things, may abound to every good work," (2 Cor. 9:8).

The Third Use. For Reproof and Admonition;

To the adversaries of Israel. Will you lift up your heads who are but as bought slaves? Look to it for if the Lord has given his Son, and he has given his blood for his people, I tell you he will even give a hundred monarchies, for them, "For I am the Lord thy God, the Holy One of Israel, thy Saviour; I gave Egypt for thy ransom, Ethiopia and Seba for thee. Thus saith the Lord, your Redeemer, the Holy One of Israel; for your sake I have sent to Babylon, and have brought down all their nobles, and; the Chaldeans, whose cry is in their ships," (Isa. 43:3, 14). The Lord calls you, who touch his inheritance, his evil neighbors, and reads your doom, "Thus saith the Lord against all mine evil neighbors, that touch the inheritance which I have caused my people Israel to inherit; Behold, I will pluck them out of their land, and pluck out the house of Judah from among them," (Jer. 12:14). Be wise, be instructed, when you remember that Zion's king is the, "King of kings, and the Lord of Lords," and is engaged against you in her quarrel.

To the despisers and neglecters of this plenteous redemption, is there such redemption offered, and dare you slight it? How can you be saved without it, or escape the punishment of such neglect?

God treasures up such mercy, and you treasure up such wrath by despising him! "Despisest thou the riches of his goodness and forbearance and long-suffering; not knowing that the goodness of God leadeth to repentance?" (Rom. 2:4). Take warning before he strikes, "Because there is wrath, beware lest he take thee away with his stroke; then a great ransom cannot deliver thee," (Job. 36:18). How many nations have been ruined by contemning this salvation; as the mariner steers his course by the direction of shelves and rocks, as well as of stars; so we should make use of what has split others.

To those who are the redeemed of the Lord. What, will you be unbelieving? Will you deal unfaithfully *to him* with whom there is plenteous redemption? Is your mind set upon the things above in this plenteous redemption? Must he say of you, "Though I have redeemed them, yet they have spoken lies against me?" If we do not find deliverance from the power of lust, if we do not find all the grace we need, the need is not *in the redemption* which is with the Lord, but in our being no more with the Lord in some way; the consolations of God are small to us, and we do not draw from its breast.

The Fourth Use. By way of Exhortation, to many that they come to the Lord with whom is plenteous redemption. Here is plenty and will not many come to the Lord? Will you forsake your own mercy? Know your encouragements, your way, and time. Obtain this pearl of great price; yes, the field where the treasure is hid. I remember that it is said of Pompey, that with a stamp of his foot he could command many thousands, and that they would run upon the most desperate dangers: and shall not one word of the Lord Jesus do as much?

To, those few that are coming. Why are you so discouraged, so halting, when such plenty is prepared? Shall the Lord draw the table› shut the door, seal the fountain, and toll your passing bell? O make haste, thou wilt not long have such plenty waiting on thee, nor be endured with such long-suffering. Surely from what has been said, some of your hearts are more than almost persuaded. But alas! I have shown you only a little: yet a shred may show you the fineness of the cloth of Arras but the opening of the whole suit would be with greater advantage of beauty. Come nearer, take hold, and its plenty will pour itself on you. Does not what you have heard suffice to take hold of jour spirits?

To those whom the Lord hath brought over to himself. Remember what there is with the Lord for you, and having high thoughts of him. This redemption is with the Lord that you may trust and fear him. Of such it is said, "O how great is thy goodness, which thou hast laid up for them that fear thee; which thou hast wrought for them that trust in thee before the sons of men!" (Psa. 31:19). Whose fault is it if *you* live poorly? Go and improve this plenty as your own, for so you may. Whatever your case is, here is that which will reach it; there is yet redemption for Israel. This redemption will raise up Israel out of all his depths, from the grave of all his sins and sorrows; will set Jerusalem on the top of the mountains, and make her a praise in the earth.

The Fifth Use. This affords plenty of *encouragement*. O how rich are those that are interested in this "plenteous redemption" that is with the Lord; and how comfortable it is to know it! "Thou, O Lord, art our father, our Redeemer; thy name is from everlasting," (Isa. 63:16). This is enough to encourage, whatever our weakness may be, "Fear not, thou worm Jacob, and ye men of Israel; I will help thee, saith the Lord, and thy Redeemer, the Holy One of Israel," (Isa.

41:14). Whatever the times are you may lift up your head, "For your redemption draweth nigh," you may, on this ground, commend yourself to the Lord in the greatest extremity, and say, "Into thine hand I commit my spirit: thou hast redeemed me, O Lord God of truth," (Psa. 31:5). You must glorify the Lord with what encouragements you have, "For ye are bought with a price: therefore glorify God in your body, and in your spirit, which are God's," (1 Cor. 6:20). What a piece of good news all this is to Zion at this day! How it should cheer us, though all seem to run headlong into confusion, though all seem dead, and such impossibilities appear on the renewing of the Lord's work, and raising up of the churches of Christ! Let no news overwhelm us while we have this word, "With him is plenteous redemption." For such things we are pressed to be *heavenly minded.*

CHAPTER 4:
PRAISE THE GLORY OF HIS GRACE

Eph. 1:6, "To the praise of the glory of his grace."

Here, the apostle is giving thanks to the Father, "for all spiritual blessings in Christ." He enumerates several particulars, and in these words mentions the design of all namely, that he might exalt "the praise of the glory of his grace," which tends to our use of being heavenly minded.

THE DOCTRINE: That it is the good pleasure of God, to work all good to his people in such a way and manner, as may be "to the praise of the glory of his grace." Every agent works to an end, and this is the end of God in all be does for his people.

I. We shall open the terms used in the text.

1. *Grace.* Grace has a peculiar notion in which it goes beyond what is proper, (in some respects) to love, or show mercy and goodness to. It denotes a special favor, where there is special reason to the contrary.

This was the case with the Jews, they dealt "proudly, and hardened their necks." "But they and our fathers dealt proudly, and hardened their necks, and hearkened not to thy commandments, And refused to obey, neither were mindful of thy wonders that thou didst among them; but hardened their necks, and in their rebellion appointed a captain to return to their bondage: but thou art a God ready to pardon, gracious and merciful, slow to anger, and of great kindness, and forsookest them not," (Neh. 9:16-17). The Lord has occasion to show forth this attribute since the fall, and it is well he chooses to magnify his grace on us, who are not only rebels, but most unkind and treacherous creatures all along.

2. It is His grace. Grace, as it is attributed to God, is in him as God, and, therefore, is in him in a far more transcendent manner, and measure, than, in all the creatures. Grace in him is increased in finite, without division, or multiplication. That grace which is the fruit of the Spirit in the saint, can pity and pardon enemies, and is more than what is in his fellows; but the grace which if in God is infinitely more, "But not as the offence, so also is the free gift. For if through the offence of one many be dead, much more the grace of

God, and the gift by grace, which is by one man, Jesus Christ, hath abounded unto many," (Rom. 5:15).

3. The Glory of his grace. A thing is in its glory, when, as the sun in its meridian on a clear day, it shines in its full strength, with all the advantage which may serve to set out its excellence. When, as Ahesuerus, resolves to let others see what he is, has, or can do. Sure little things, or a little of anything, will not suffice to set out the glory of the grace of God how able he is to pardon and make happy such wretches as we are. Therefore when he would show his glory to Moses, he proclaimed his name, "The Lord, the Lord God, merciful and gracious, long suffering, and abundant in goodness and truth," (Exod. 34:6).

4. The Praise of the glory of his grace. That is, that his grace might so appear and work, that men and angels might have occasion and ability to make heaven and earth resound with its praises for ever; that his wondrous works this way might be talked of by every tongue, "They shall abundantly utter the memory of thy great goodness, and shall sing of thy righteousness. The Lord is gracious and full of compassion; slow to anger, and of great mercy," (Psa. 145:7-8). The distributive justice of God is praiseworthy, in that good he does for

his people; but his grace is quite another thing, and is more exalted. God's great determinate end in all, is, " to the praise of the glory of his grace."

II.   We shall a little more explain that the design of God lies in this that things are laid for the purpose of showing "the praise of the glory of his grace," and how this appears.

1.   In the counsels of his grace for his people. That he should purpose such good for souls, for such an end, and find out such a way for its accomplishment; that God should set his thoughts in this way to work about mankind; that he should make way for the execution of those thoughts by Jesus Christ; and that he should do all in such a manner as might best commend his grace to us, this is "to the praise of the glory of his grace: according as he hath chosen us in him before the foundation of the world, that we should be holy and without blame before him in love," (Eph. 1:4). "Who hath saved us, and called us with a holy calling, not according to our works, but according to his own purpose and grace, which was given us in Christ Jesus before the world began," (2 Tim. 1:9). "God so loved the world, that he gave his only begotten Son, that whosoever believeth in him should not perish, but

have everlasting life," (John 3:16). Surely, we may cry out, "O! the depth of the riches both of the wisdom and knowledge of God!" Let it sweetly astonish your spirits. God has not only consulted this grace for men when they were not, but when he knew what they would be. They *were not*, and so could not move him; he knew what rebels they would prove, and so might move him only to the contrary; he saw us in our blood when we were, "cast out in the open field to the loathing of our persons," He could have kept out sin, but it was let into the world that his grace might have the greater triumph, "Where sin abounded, grace did much more abound," (Rom. 5:20).

The grace of God to his people appears, in that he should design saving grace to them, and them *only*. Out of his good pleasure he has determined the persons, the end, and the means; though it must be granted that all his *in a sort* partake of grace. It would be a sad blemish if we should admit such a flaw in this case as some would have us; it would be a desperate hazard if we should suffer such a stone to be loosened in the foundation, "And he said, I will make all my goodness to pass before thee, and I will proclaim the name of the Lord before thee; and will be gracious to whom I will be gracious, and will show mercy on whom I will show mercy," (Exod. 33:19). "Even so then at this present time also, there is a remnant, according to the election of grace," (Rom. 11:5). "Nevertheless the foundation of God standeth sure, having this seal, the Lord knoweth them that are his," (2 Tim. 2:19). These, and many other passages plainly assert the doctrine of *election*.

2. Consider the outward workings of these counsels of grace for his people, in making, preserving, and governing the world for his people, and prosecuting his gracious design. Though the Lord has subordinate ends in the expressions of his mercy, and justice, to the world, yet the last end is to the praise of his glorious grace, "For all things are for your sakes, that the abundant grace might, through the thanksgiving of many, redound to the glory of God," (2 Cor. 4:15). I tell you God would not suffer this world to continue a moment, but on this account, and he will order things, strangely as they may seem to go, that they will fall into this purpose. If any man considers, he may apprehend that things are designed for a higher end than what is obvious to sense; but a believer apprehends what that higher end is, what is hevenly,

and knows, "that all things work together for good, to them that love God, to them who ate the called according to his purpose," (Rom. 8:28). Let us adore the glory of his grace, who manages all things to show forth his praise. Surely all the works of God may praise his goodness, but saints have further occasion and capacity to, "praise the glory of his grace."

The, "glory of his grace," appears in the manner of communicating this design, and its way to men. God not only provided for the display of his grace, and concluded with our Savior before man was, but when man had a being, had such a need, and deserved so contrary, before man could ask or think such a thing, he revealed it and engaged himself. In this way he dealt with our first parents who had brought themselves and us into such a condition. The Lord came to them before night, and includes in his sad sermon this use of consolation, "I will put enmity between thee (*the serpent*) and the woman, and between thy seed and her seed; he shall, bruise thy head, and thou shalt bruise his heel," (Gen. 3:15). Indeed such is his grace, that he in this way prevents every people, where the word of this grace comes; "I am sought of them that asked not for me; I am found of them that sought me not: I said, behold me, behold me, unto a nation that was not called by my name," (Isa. 65:1). That he might show, "the glory of his grace," he was so free as to reveal the Lord Jesus, and the effect of his coming long before; and, what is still more, he did not leave himself free, but engaged himself by promise, that we might have its comfort so long beforehand, and be assured of it.

The "glory of his grace" is seen, in bringing on the design by degrees, through all its impediments and apparent deaths. How often did all seem to be lost in the low condition of the church, and of David's family! Yet, in the fullness of time, it broke out in all the fullness of grace, "The word was made flesh, and dwelt among us, and we beheld his glory, the glory as of the only begotten of the Father, full of grace and truth," (John 1:14). God did not forget his promise during the many thousand years before it was accomplished, nor could anything fall out to violate his word. This manner of proceeding gradually, in such way of difficulty, conduces much to set forth the glory of the grace of God, "Who art thou O great mountain? before Zerubbabel thou shalt become a plain, add he shall bring forth the head-stone thereof with shoutings, crying, grace, grace unto it," (Zech. 4:7). No wonder there were such rejoicings, and praises sung, both by the heavenly host, and by the saints on earth, when the gospel "day-spring from on high" visited them,

Behold the "glory of his grace," in completing the work of grace and glory in Jesus Christ. The people of God are humbled and exalted in him, have fulfilled all righteousness in him, and received all glory in him. They have obeyed and suffered in him; they are justified, adopted, crucified, and sanctified with him; yes, set in heavenly places together with him. In this has the grace of God abounded, not only to those of that generation, but to generations succeeding, "That in the ages to come he might show the exceeding riches of his grace, in his kindness towards us, through Christ Jesus," (Eph. 2:7). All was transacted and finished in Christ, as a common person, and as our surety.

III. The glory of this grace yet further appears, in what it does for the people of God.

1. The grace of God works upon the worst of sinners. It does not manifest itself as grace, to such characters, until it has convinced them they are the *worst* of sinners; and then it does not leave them in that condition, but subdues and renews them. Grace brings them under it, and brings their corruptions under, "For

sin shall not have dominion over you: for ye are not under the law, but under grace," (Rom. 6:14). Scripture and experience testify, that God will work on those that are very unlikely, to let us see he can work any way. Grace may put on a visor, and rake great troubles in the soul, but the design is gracious. It may in this way appear at first, that afterward it may show itself so much the more to be grace; for such are our frames, that grace would not be so glorious if it did not scare us a little. However, it does not leave us there, it afterwards heals and comforts, " The Spirit of the Lord God is upon me; because the Lord hath anointed me to preach good tidings unto the meek; he hath sent me to bind up the brokenhearted, to proclaim liberty to the captives, and the opening of the prison to them that are bound; to proclaim the acceptable year of the Lord, and the day of vengeance of our God; to comfort all that mourn," (Isa. 61:1-2).

2. The grace of God works on sinners being dead, and its pleasure determines their choice when they are enemies. "And you hath he quickened who were dead in trespasses and sins; for by grace are ye: saved, through faith; and that not of yourselves: it is the gift of God," (Eph. 2:1, 8). "Thy people shall be willing

in the day of thy power," (Psa. 110:3). "So then it is not of him that willeth, nor of him that runneth, but of God that showeth mercy," (Rom. 9:16). The grace of God works a death; or rather a sense of death, and aversion to sin, which is the beginning of spiritual life; and it proceeds to melt, persuade, change, heal, and refresh the heart. This grace of life may be long, and work in the soul, before it makes its appearance; as the unborn child has a principle of life before it is seen to live: therefore do not let soul-modesty strangle it by doubting.

3. The grace of God accepts and pardons sinners, in, and for the sake of, another and accepts their workings, though weak and full of mixture, on the same account. "He hath made us accepted in the beloved and n by the obedience ˗of one shall many be made righteous." "Let us therefore come boldly unto the throne of grace, that we may obtain mercy, and find grace to help in time of need." We would have the crown of glory set on the head of grace in us, but we must cast it at his feet, or, rather set it on the head of grace as it is in God; he will not give the glory of this his grace to another, it is enough if we have the benefit.

4. The glory of divine grace appears, in maintaining and carrying on the work, notwithstanding the remainders of sin, power of temptation, and weakness of means; as if the sufficiency of grace, and the perfect power of it, could not shine forth but in this way. "My grace is sufficient for thee; for my strength is made perfect in weakness," (2 Cor. 12:9). The Lord suffers such temptations and weaknesses to fall in at our coming out of bondage, and to clog all our wilderness way, that his grace may obtain a name. The cry shall be "grace! grace!" to the adding of the very top-stone. Grace will be glorious in preserving and nourishing this plant, though such weeds grow about it, such storms assault it, and all other helps desert it.

5. The whole matter is so graciously assured, that it redounds, "to the praise of the glory of his grace," and presses us to be heavenly minded. Indeed, grace is sure from its freeness, riches, order, and engagement. "It is of faith, that it might be by grace; to the end the promise might be sure to all the seed," (Rom. 4:16). Grace has a mighty efficacy to establish the heart, where it is revealed; and God has appointed ordinances also, on purpose to assure us that we might have strong

consolation, and that he might have great glory. He has appointed two sacraments to set forth, and confirm his grace to us. In this the Holy Spirit is not only a teacher but a witness. *The Lord first assures the thing*, then the person, and, when it may be for the glory of his grace, we shall have the assurance of it as to ourselves.

6. The glory of his grace is seen in converting, grace into glory. The soul's great mercy is at once perfected, when grace is ripened into glory. Then the glory of grace will appear, and there will be matter and power of eternal praise. Then will the soul look back and see, those mysteries of grace it could not so well understand before; it will look forward and behold what it was impossible to see before.

We may not inquire into the *Reason* of this doctrine, so our Lord Jesus seems to intimate in his reply to Judas, when he said, "Lord how is it thou wilt manifest thyself unto us, and not unto the World?" (John 14:22). Or, we must resolve all into this, "Even so, Father: for so it seemed good in thy sight," or, say as Micah, because, " he delighteth in mercy," for the way of his grace sets out all his other perfections most fully.

The First Use. It informs us what is indeed the doctrine of grace, which is, the doctrine of the gospel;

or, as it is called, "the gospel of the grace of God," That which holds forth the glory of grace, and which is to the praise of its glory, that is the doctrine of grace; but that which fails in either is not according to the gospel. This may serve us as a clue, to lead us through the labyrinth of errors on both sides.

Some, on one hand advances the creature, nature, and works too high, and so dethrones grace from its glory; "If it be of works, then it is no more grace," Christ is not Christ to them who advance the creature. He "is become of no effect unto you, whosoever of you are justified by the law," (Gal. 5:4). Christ teaches other doctrine than this, when he says, "So likewise ye, when ye shall have done all those things which are commanded you, say, we are unprofitable servants," (Luke 17:10). The Apostle also speaks the same thing, when he says, "Not of works lest any man should boast," The experience which is sound declares the same, its language is, "We are all as an unclean thing, and all our righteousnesses are as filthy rags." Maintain a spirit of jealousy against that image of jealous men are laboring to set up, as well as to the doctrine itself.

You may perhaps object, that men of great reason and parts go that way, against which you speak. To this I would answer, that as the matter revealed is a mystery, so the manner of revealing is mysterious. Grace revealed the scriptures, and must reveal them to us, or we shall understand carnally, and err damnably. Flesh and blood must not be consulted, the wisdom of this is enmity, and the Lord, in the whole of this design, sets himself to confound the wise and confute the dispute. We must plough with the Lord's heifer, if we would find out the riddle; the Spirit of God is the best doctor, and the unction of it the best teaching. A mean spade may find a rich mine; so the Lord often hides "from the wise and prudent," what he reveals "unto babes." I hope I am speaking to those who are not under a temptation to despise sanctified learning in officers or others.

Other persons, on the other hand, advance grace, so as not to the praise of its glory; while some would pluck it from the throne, others would tread it in the mire, and turn it to negligence and lasciviousness. To this it may be objected, that they have such excellent strains of the grace of God, and of making every thing good. These notions must be tried and sifted; for they may be but to set off something worse, as the monks hate many notable strains of self-denial and love to God. Respect must be had to qualifications and duties, in their place, else all grace will be abused, and all profaneness introduced; such monstrous issues have been in the world. We must therefore be more cautious. I said we must have respect to them in their place; yet they may not be idolized. All graces and duties are to be considered as they flow from Christ or lead to him, and as they are, "to the praise of the glory of his grace." Observe the Apostle's exhortation, "This is a faithful saying, and these things I will that thou affirm constantly, that they which have believed in God might be careful to maintain good works. These things are good and profitable unto men," (Titus 3:8). As the Apostle Peter testifies, "That this is the true grace of God wherein ye stand," so do I, that the doctrine which is held forth in our confession, is the true doctrine of the grace of God, against errors from the one hand and on the other.

The Second Use. It shows us the true work of grace;—the goings of God in the sanctuary and in our hearts. Surely the pure stream of this work flows from the fountain of grace in God, and directly takes this course, that is, "to the praise of the glory of his grace." Though it seems sometimes to run under ground, and at other times to fetch a compass; it leaves upon the spirit of a man, a deep and everlasting tincture of admiring the grace of God and the nature of godliness.

It detects common workings of common grace. You are but in yourself, your workings and notions are to the praise and glory of self; there you do begin and end. You may be carried very high, and yet remain in yourself; and like a lark fall down as a stone. The grace of God must ravish you out of yourself in what you are and do, both as to first principle and last end, or you are undone; there must be no, "confidence in the flesh."

It detects, also, that work which talks much of grace, but is not attended with what may show forth its praises. It does not wear the livery of the grace of God, but the devil's badge. If the grace of God brings you salvation, it will teach you, "that denying ungodliness and worldly lust, we should live soberly, righteously, and godly, in this present world," (Titus 2:12). Consider grace either is to its doctrine or work it is a mystery, and is compared to the wind blowing, and the child in the womb; but the sense and fruit in gracious hearts bring much light in the case.

The Third Use. It shows us our great duty and miscarriages on both hands.

1. That we look on this great design of God, his method in it, and labor to promote it to our utmost, in all his dealings with us, and our receivings, from him: for we greatly wrong the Lord and ourselves if we do not do this, and are not heavenly minded.

We have a great duty to observe, in exalting his grace eminently and ultimately among his attributes, though not only. We must honor his holiness and justice, but his grace must keep the throne; for he is exalted to be gracious. It is necessary that the creature is debased and emptied, its glory blasted, and its beauty stained. We must not glory after the flesh, nor even know Christ after the flesh, we must take no rest short of this grace, as it is in God and in its glory.

2. Let us praise the glory of his grace. We may be an astonishment to ourselves, that we are not in a continual ecstasy at such grace. Shall not such monuments of grace be instruments of its praise? It is all we have to glory in and to glorify, "He that glorieth, let him glory in the Lord," (1 Cor. 1:31). This is the theme on which we should ever dwell. Surely the Lord would rather have his glory than his majesty exalted.

Let us then say to our glory, awake! and when we have said all, we must conclude, he, "is exalted above all blessing and praise." O how would this stir up others, and so we should praise him with many mouth?

3. Let us not only talk, but be, and walk, "to the praise of the glory of his grace." Let us live a life of faith, that we may be what we are by it, to its praise: it was so with Paul, "By the grace of God I am what I am: and his grace which was bestowed upon me was not in vain; but I laboured more abundantly than they all: yet not I, but the grace of God which was with me," (1 Cor. 15:10). It may be so with us, "God is able to make all grace abound toward you; that ye, always having all-sufficiency in all things, may abound to every good work," (2 Cor. 9:8). Let us also live a life of love, holiness, and cheerfulness. Our whole conversation must be regulated and sweetened by it, "For our rejoicing is this, the testimony of our conscience, that in simplicity and godly sincerity, not with fleshly wisdom, but by the grace of God, we have had our conversation in the world," (2 Cor. 1:12). Let us set this as our highest spark at which we should aim. Let us not receive the grace of God in vain, but be devoted to it. Faith, indeed, hits the mark, but love and cheerful

obedience are as feathers to the arrows. Let us live a life of usefulness. As we must be good receivers, so let us be, "good stewards of the grace of God." Let us hold ourselves as vessels of honor prepared for the master's use. It is a great talent committed to us, and calls for great trading. It will not excuse us in the day of accounts that we denied our talents, or that we thought we had none.

The Fourth Use. It affords unspeakable encouragements to the Lord's poor worms, who are admirers of the grace of God, and desire to be to the praise of its glory. I think when the church of God has heard such glad tidings as these, she should never be more afraid of evil ones. If Zion's physician this day seeks himself glory and praise for doing great cures, and on free cost, he has occasion enough. Consider, souls, it is the grace of God that must be in this way glorified; he is, "God and not man." You are not to expect such poor pity from him as from a sorry man: for he has a multitude of tender mercies. Consider God's design is successful and most sweet, "My counsel must stand, and I will do all my pleasure." You may hope he has a gracious design towards you if your design is toward him if unbelief and unkindness are a trouble, and you desire to live, "as becometh the gospel of Christ." Now, beloved, "I commend you to God, and to the word of his grace," that you have, continually, high thoughts of him and his Son, that you might be, always, heavenly minded.